MIND YOGA
THE SIMPLE SOLUTION TO STRESS
THAT YOU'VE NEVER HEARD BEFORE*

*NO STRETCHY PANTS REQUIRED

MARY SCHILLER

www.maryschiller.com

ISBN: 0692709452
ISBN-13: 978-0692709450

DEDICATION

To Sydney Banks, whose expression of the Three Principles
transformed my life.

CONTENTS

ACKNOWLEDGEMENT

For my mother, Lucille, whose light still shines in my heart.

INTRODUCTION
A WHOLE NEW SOLUTION TO STRESS

The last time I googled "stress relief," I came up with 5 million results. "Stress management" gave me 8 million results.

Millions and millions of articles, videos, audios ... and are they telling us anything we haven't already heard before?

I'm about to make the first of many bold assertions in this book. What you're about to discover is a radically new contribution to the conversation about stress: a completely different way to solve this problem – and solve it for good.

I know it sounds impossible. Maybe even ridiculous. When I first came upon what I'll share with you, I was as skeptical as anyone. As you'll see in the first chapter, I had a long and messy history with stress. I didn't believe that anything could help me feel the kind of peace and clarity that I longed for.

"Longed for" is a nice way of saying that I would have given anything to have just one stress-free day. I paid a lot of money during my life to get that one stress-free day, and it never happened.

Now, I have an essentially stress-free *life*. Wow. I can't believe I wrote that sentence and it's actually true.

What I'm going to tell you flies in the face of everything we've all been taught about stress: what it is, and what we can do about it. I've taken what I've learned, what I've taught to other people, and what I've experienced for myself and created what I've called Mind Yoga.

Mind Yoga is a simple and effective stress relief method that anyone, of any age, can learn. It doesn't involve anything physical, so you don't need a yoga mat or a gym membership.

It doesn't require learning any techniques, so there is nothing for you to memorize or practice.

What is Mind Yoga? It's a simple understanding of the real cause of stress that up until now has been invisible to you. Once you see what's actually going on behind the curtain, your entire experience of stress will shift into low gear, and eventually it will fade into the background so as to have no effect on the quality of your life.

You'll find yourself more relaxed as well as more energized, better able to make decisions, more productive and much more creative. The benefits of Mind Yoga are endless.

In short, *you'll be free*: to live the life you really want to live, free of the impact of stress.

Don't believe me just yet? That's OK. I invite you to keep reading. Let's start with how I was living before I discovered the principles behind Mind Yoga. As you'll see, it was not a pretty place to be ...

CHAPTER 1
MY "HATE AFFAIR" WITH STRESS

Ah, stress. Sometimes I feel like I should capitalize it, Stress, like a name. For most of my adult life, stress had its own persona, as if we were in a relationship together: a dysfunctional and tumultuous relationship, with no love lost between us.

Stress and I were in a "hate affair." I should have broken off the relationship earlier – and I would have, if I had known how. I tried everything I could think of to end it, but like a stalker, stress kept showing up and wreaking havoc in my life.

Do you remember when you first started to feel like stress was an inevitable, inextricable part of your life?

Here's how my relationship with stress began ...

When someone tells you that you have a mental illness, it kind of throws you for a loop. The first time I realized that I had been labeled as "mentally ill" was shortly after I separated from my first husband in 1990. I was 29 years old, and all I knew for sure was that I had survived a violent marriage and had escaped with my life and my then-toddler daughter. When I drove away from that house, away from him and the marriage, I thought my problems were over.

I had no idea that there was something else that I needed to try to escape from, too.

Leading up to the day I left, I had spent seven long years trying to figure out what I was doing that was "causing" my ex-husband to treat me the way he did. I had never experienced any sort of violence or abuse before, and those seven years were the most challenging of my life. I lived day to day with the stress of trying to figure out how to stay alive and timing my eventual exit.

Then in 1990, the violence took on a whole new hue, and I knew I had to get out or risk my daughter not having her mother anymore. I made a hasty plan to leave, and one morning after my ex-husband went to work, I got in my Volvo with my daughter in the back seat and all the necessities I could fit in the trunk, and I headed for the freeway.

I filed for divorce four days later. My attorney recommended that I see a counselor who specialized in treating women who had endured domestic violence. At that time, I had just barely started to put the words "domestic violence" into context. I had never seen my marriage in that way, believe it or not. I was so focused on staying alive and keeping my daughter safe, I hadn't had time to step back and see what was really happening. It seemed like a good idea to talk with an expert so that I could gain some clarity about everything I had been through.

The counselor, Gail, was a nice, if slightly rumpled, woman who saw clients at her sunny, comfortable home. I attended a few group meetings and a couple of one-to-one sessions. As I talked with Gail, I began to notice how tense I was most of the time – something that had been invisible to me over the course of the marriage.

During one of the private sessions, Gail said to me, "Mary, most women like you, with post-traumatic stress disorder, can learn to cope quite well." She went on to say that because of the particular types of abuse that I endured, she didn't feel she was qualified to help me. She intimated that my particular brand of PTSD was more than she could take on.

I remember thinking, "What does that mean? How sick am I, anyway?"

By the time I saw my final psychotherapist in 2012 – shortly before I discovered what I will share with you in this book – I had seen upwards of twenty-five different mental health professionals.

And I didn't feel at peace. I was still in a committed relationship with Stress, with a capital "S."

I had moments where I was reasonably fine, and I generally functioned all right. But I also had emotional outbursts, and I had periods of major anxiety where I felt completely out of control and overwhelmed. I flinched when people came near me, and I never, ever relaxed.

Even worse, it seemed like stress was clouding my ability to see who I was and what I really wanted from life. I would have given anything – *anything* – if someone could have shown me how to find, and hold onto, inner peace.

The physical toll of all this stress was obvious, as well, particularly in some severe problems I was having with my spine. It was like the weight of the stress was so great, my body couldn't hold me up.

Because of what I had heard from all the psychological professionals over the years, I believed that the traumatic events I went through were causing all the stress. I also saw that my thinking had something to do with it, but I didn't know what to do about my thoughts. They seemed unmanageable, like children who wouldn't do what I told them to do.

It also looked like there were external stress "triggers" all around me: certain sounds (like kids crying) and types of people (especially those who liked to yell a lot). I couldn't watch movies that reminded me of the violence I experienced. I tried to avoid all of these "triggers" as best I could.

At my core, I was afraid to look too closely at myself. I felt like a broken person, and I constantly questioned my judgment and my abilities. I didn't know if it was really safe to be me.

In addition to all the counseling, I used every technique I came across to deal with stress, from self-hypnosis and meditation to positive thinking and Emotional Freedom Technique (tapping). I never took any prescription medication, but I began looking into a drug that was in clinical trials to help people with PTSD.

In 2013, I felt pretty desperate.

As much as I tried to, I couldn't accept that my PTSD symptoms were, indeed, permanent. Even though I had been fighting with stress for nearly three decades by then, something kept pushing me to look for yet another solution.

I had some happy times during all those years. I got remarried, I had some good jobs and I enjoyed being a mother to my daughter. But something was missing.

I simply could not believe that stress was an inevitable part of my life – more like the foundation of my life. I looked around at other people who were happy, people who hadn't been through something traumatic, and I was consumed with jealousy. When they would stress out over seemingly minor things – like their job or their noisy neighbor or whatever – I would get angry. How could they let something like that bother them when I was dealing with real stress?

Looking back on all this now, I can see, to borrow the title of the movie, that I was absolutely, if innocently, clueless.

Forget what all the experts had told me over the years: I see very clearly now that my understanding of stress – both in myself and in other people – was completely upside down and backwards.

In early 2014, I discovered what I had been searching for: the ultimate solution for stress.

Hang onto your chair, because I'm about to make another bold claim. What I share in this book is the only effective and permanent solution to stress. **Once you see what stress actually is, stress holds no power over you.**

Just a few weeks after discovering this solution for myself, I broke off my hate affair with stress, and my PTSD symptoms dissolved without effort. This, after nearly thirty years of dealing with those symptoms and feeling like I was unfixable.

What really gets me is that it's so obvious and so simple, I can't believe I didn't hear about it sooner. I remember thinking, "Other people knew about this, so why didn't someone tell me about it before now?"

I'm going to be that "someone" for you. I'll tell you what no one has ever told you about stress that will allow you to break off your relationship with it for good ...

CHAPTER 2
WHAT IS CAUSING STRESS IN YOUR LIFE?

It probably doesn't take you long to answer the question in this chapter's title. So let's make a list.

What are the events, situations, people, places and so forth that routinely bring up those familiar – and uncomfortable – feelings of frustration, anger, bodily tension or exhaustion? Write them here or on another sheet of paper.

If you're anything like I was, the list of stressors felt like the lyrics to a familiar song, repeating over and over again like a broken record (yes, I'm old enough to remember LPs).

Here's a sample of what my life stressors looked like:

- The traumatic events in my first marriage
- Trauma "triggers," like standing or sitting too close to an unfamiliar man or hearing people arguing loudly
- The lack of direction in my work life, which looked like a random hodgepodge of advanced degrees and jobs rather than a career
- My second husband (to whom I'm still married, I'm happy to say), with all his habits that sometimes seemed endearing but also drove me crazy
- My health and in particular, my spine, which was a constant source of worry
- My inability to feel at peace, a stressor in and of itself
- My lack of freedom in what I did with my time, which was consumed by too much work and not enough time off to enjoy my life

There were more, but those were some of the biggies for me. They remind me of what two psychiatrists, Thomas Holmes and Richard Rahe, put forth as the Holmes and Rahe Stress Scale. In their research, Holmes and Rahe examined medical records of upwards of 5,000 people to see if there was a correlation between life events, stress and visits to doctors. In addition, they asked patients to rank certain life stressors and conducted other research to see if stress correlated to medical problems.

I won't include the whole scale since it amounts to 43 different stressors, but here are the top 20, according to Holmes and Rahe. I've marked the ones I've experienced:

1. Death of a spouse
2. Divorce: yes
3. Marital separation: yes
4. Imprisonment
5. Death of a close family member: yes
6. Personal injury or illness: yes
7. Marriage: yes (twice)
8. Dismissal from work
9. Marital reconciliation: yes
10. Retirement

11. Change in health of family member: yes

12. Pregnancy: yes

13. Sexual difficulties: yes

14. Gain a new family member: yes

15. Business readjustment: yes

16. Change in financial state: yes

17. Death of a close friend

18. Change to different line of work: yes

19. Change in frequency of arguments: yes

20. Major mortgage: yes

The Holmes and Rahe Stress Scale also was said to predict the likelihood of medical problems as a result of these stressors, and they even developed a stress scale for children under 18 years of age (with events like death of a parent and unplanned pregnancy). As far as I can tell, this stress scale is still in use today, nearly 50 years after it was developed.

According to Merriam Webster, stress is "a state of mental tension and worry caused by problems in your life, work, etc.; something that causes strong feelings of worry or anxiety." This definition is explaining stress as a state of feeling: something we're experiencing on an emotional level.

Is it any wonder that we feel hopeless in the face of stress?

All of this paints a bleak picture of managing stress in our lives. Most of those stressors are inevitable or out of our control. (Do you know anyone who can avoid illness, for example?) So are we all just destined to stay in this relationship with stress forever, 'til death do us part?

The answer is an absolute and unequivocal *No*.

We are neither destined nor designed to live our lives dominated by, or even particularly impacted by, stress.

Does that sound strange to you? It did to me, at first. But now it's really obvious to me – and this is what Mind Yoga is all about – that we do not have to accept that stress is a natural and inevitable by-product of modern life.

The next chapter will teach you the first "pose" of Mind Yoga, which will reveal that everything we've been talking about in terms of "stressors" is completely and utterly wrong.

And that is the best news ever, because it brings hope back into our relationship with stress: hope that stress can, and will, subside.

By the way, Mind Yoga doesn't require wearing stretchy pants, so no need to change into them (unless you want to, of course) …

CHAPTER 3
MIND YOGA POSE 1: LOOK INSIDE

At the end of the previous chapter, I said that everything we have been told and everything we believe about stress is wrong. Why? Two reasons:

First, because if we really knew what caused stress and what took care of stress, most of us wouldn't be these tightly wound-up stress balls.

And second, because in 2014, someone finally showed me the truth about stress: what it is, and what to do about it.

What I heard was so radically different from everything else out there, and it was so incredibly simple, at first I didn't believe it.

So I tested it. And I tested it again. Rinse and repeat. Until eventually, it was obvious to me that it was correct.

That's what I'd like you to do.

Don't just believe me. I've made this book brief and concise so that it's easy for you to read through it and then test what I'm saying. Experiment with it.

It goes without saying that stress – the emotional and physical experience – is not healthy for us.

You probably have lots of personal examples of how stress is adversely affecting you. Perhaps you're not feeling as healthy as you want to, or your overall mental state is low. Maybe a relationship is suffering, or you're not able to move forward in certain areas of your life. What are some ways that stress is affecting you? Write them here or on a separate piece of paper:

What became clear over the course of my "hate affair" with stress was that even a tiny amount of it was detrimental to me. It made my mind foggy, I couldn't make good decisions and I felt physically unsteady. With a slight *zing* of stress, my whole body would freeze up, or my emotions would take over and frustration would stop me in my tracks. My creativity suffered, which was particularly upsetting since writing on deadline formed the foundation of my work life.

Where have we gone wrong?
We've all been looking in the wrong direction.

We've been looking to places, events and people as the sources of stress. **That's why pose 1 of Mind Yoga is so simple: Look inside.**

Look away from where you've always thought stress is coming from, and look in a new direction.

What I'm about to say is going to strike you as odd at first, and that's OK. When I first heard it, it took me a while to understand it fully. But as you keep reading, please also keep an open mind.

We'll begin with where stress does not come from.

Stress does not come from divorce.

Stress does not come from a change in your finances.

Stress does not come from a loved one dying.

Stress does not come from a mortgage.

Stress does not come from dealing with bad drivers.

Stress does not come from interacting with other people.

Stress does not come from a health condition.

Stress does not come from a place.

And so on.

Not only that ...

There is no such thing as a stressful job.

There is no such thing as a stressful situation.

There is no such thing as a stressful relationship.

There is no such thing as a stressful event.

There is no such thing as a stressful time of life.

There is no such thing as a stressful conversation.

There is no such thing as a stressful illness.

There is no such thing as a stressful environment.

And so on.

I know this sounds really different from the traditional talk about stress, but that's the point. **We're about to go into Mind Yoga pose 1 and look in a brand new direction ...**

Stress does not come *at* us, nor does it come *from* anything or anyone.

There is no mechanism that carries stress from something or someone, and toward and into us. For example, stress is not like a germ; we cannot "catch" stress from a conversation, a relationship, a situation, an environment or a person. It can look that way, but just because something looks a certain way doesn't mean it's true. The earth may look flat from certain angles, but does that mean it is?

Let's consider it logically for a moment. Where would stress actually be if, for example, it came from a job? How would stress "live" in a job? Would it live in the job description? In the building? And would it come to us via the papers we're pushing? Could other people somehow magically transmit stress to us?

You might say, "Well, if someone else is stressed, it rubs off on me."

It might look that way, but again, just because something looks true doesn't mean that it is. Here's an example. Your stressed-out and angry boss yells at you, and then you feel angry and upset. The boss didn't cause the stress. Thoughts inside your own mind caused the feeling you're experiencing. If you didn't have the thought, or if you had the thought but didn't care about having it, you wouldn't feel stressed.

Test it: Do you know people who don't get stressed out by angry bosses who yell, and instead they brush it off and go about their business? Does your boss ever get angry and for whatever reason that particular day, it doesn't bother you? That's because the boss who yells isn't creating the feeling of stress.

Also, let's say I was visiting you that day at work and heard the boss yelling. If stress were indeed "catching," then I would feel it, too. But I don't – because I don't have a thought that tells me I should feel stressed, or if I do have that thought, it's at such a low volume level that I don't even hear it.

When I started to examine the traditional explanation of stress more closely, which had seemed so real to me for my entire adult life, it fell apart instantly – because it just doesn't make any sense. I admit that I was embarrassed and a little shocked to discover the truth, which was so simple and obvious that I was stunned that I'd never seen it before.

Stress only ever comes from one place: inside our own minds.

We do not absorb stress. We do not get stressed out by things, people, events and so forth "out there." Nothing has the ability to trigger or create stress in us – except our own thinking.

We feel stressed when we have thoughts telling us we should be stressed, and we agree with them.

I'll repeat that last sentence because it's the foundation of Mind Yoga pose 1: We feel stressed when we have thoughts telling us we should be stressed, and we agree with them. And we don't actually have to agree with them!

Here's another way of saying that: Stress – in the way that we're used to thinking of it – does not actually exist. It's not a thing "out there" that we have to "deal with."

What's really happening is this: we have some thinking, we react to it as stressful, and then we have a feeling that we call "stress." On top of that, we often worry and get fearful when we have the feeling we've labeled "stress," so we go even further down that stressful road.

Thoughts and feelings are nearly identical, like two sides of the same coin. We have a thought, and that thought is reflected immediately in the feeling that comes along with it. It happens so quickly that it appears like the stress is coming at us from a thing, person, situation or event "out there." But it never works that way.

Our feelings never come from anything but our thoughts.

Feelings don't come from the past or future, and feelings only do one thing: reflect our thinking in that particular moment. When I really saw this for myself, it was like a curtain had been pulled back on the inner workings of my mind.

When people say, "I'm stressing myself out," they're absolutely right.

When people say, "You're stressing me out" or "This situation is stressing me out," they're living with a misunderstanding of where stress is coming from.

Here's an easy way of seeing all this more distinctly. I'd like you to revisit the list you wrote while reading chapter 2 – the one with all the aspects of your life that are stressful. After having just read this portion of the book, what do you see as the real source of stress in each instance?

Here's my list with the true sources of stress:

The traumatic events in my first marriage: These events only lived in the present because I had thinking about them and was paying attention to that thinking, believing it was significant and important. Along with that thinking came stress and suffering that I created innocently within myself.

Trauma "triggers," like standing or sitting too close to an unfamiliar person or hearing people arguing loudly: These "triggers" were thoughts in and of themselves. I had a thought of, "Oh, that person is standing close to me." Then I reacted to that thought by giving it credence as a threat, and then I felt stressed.

The lack of direction in my work life, which looked like a random hodgepodge of advanced degrees and jobs rather than a career: The whole notion of a "lack of direction" was a story I told myself over and over again and believed was true. Every time it popped into my head, I listened to it and felt tense.

My second husband (to whom I'm still married, I'm happy to say), with all his habits that sometimes seemed endearing but also drove me crazy: The reason his habits changed from endearing to crazy-making and back again had nothing to do with his habits and everything to do with my naturally fluctuating thoughts.

My health and in particular, my spine, which was a constant source of worry: I noticed that the less weight I gave worrisome thinking, the less often it bothered me and the fewer problems I had with my spine.

My inability to feel at peace, a stressor in and of itself:
I'll get into this in depth in a later chapter, but right now I can
say that I was also wrong about where the feeling of peace
came from. Innocently, I didn't know that peace was present
within me all along.

**My lack of freedom in what I did with my time, which
was consumed by too much work and not enough time
off to enjoy my life:** I couldn't see that I was actually already
free. Everything I heard in my head that said otherwise was a
thought-created, non-existent prison I had created for and
within myself.

Can you see, either through my list or your own, that we
had been looking in the wrong direction for the source of
stress? No matter what is happening "out there," the only
thing we're ever experiencing is what's "in here" – inside our
own minds.

In living with this understanding for a while now, I have
experienced a sense of freedom that I've never had before
because *I've realized that I can encounter anyone or anything and never
be a victim of circumstance or of another person.*

I'll give you an example from my own life – or rather, my husband's life. In a recent full-time job he held, a woman with quite a reputation for being a bully was hired to be his supervisor. For reasons we still don't understand, after being let go by the organization previously she was hired back and became my husband's boss.

Right from the start, she treated my husband, Jeff, the same way she had treated previous subordinates. She seemed to be doing everything in her power to make him miserable. And for a time, it worked – until Jeff began to understand the principles that underscore Mind Yoga.

He started to see two key things: first, that if he had thoughts about her, he could simply choose not to react to them (Mind Yoga pose 2, coming up shortly); and second, that she was reacting to her own thinking, and not to anything he was or wasn't doing.

For instance, if she assigned him work to do and his thoughts were, "This is so stupid! Why would she make me do this?", then Jeff could see where the stress was coming from: his own thinking, not her or the tasks she assigned to him. The more he was able to see that his reactions to his thoughts were causing his stress and not his boss, the more quickly his stress level went from being sky high to barely noticeable. He no longer talked about "what she had done to him" when he came home from work because he didn't see it that way anymore.

And then something else happened. His boss started to soften around the edges. Her behavior began to change, and she increasingly left him alone to do his work without interference. When Jeff eventually left that job, she actually hugged him – something that a year before would have seemed absolutely impossible.

Time after time, I've also seen that I don't have to change anything – my job, my marriage or even my health in any way at all – to live without stress.

I have dumped my "hate affair" with stress forever.

You may be asking yourself, "If stressful feelings come from my thoughts, should I change my thoughts or try to stop certain thoughts? I don't want to stress myself out anymore."

The answer is an absolute *No*. In fact, the more we try to manage or change our thinking, the worse the stressful feeling gets. You'll see why shortly.

So what do we do?

Chapter 4 will take you into the next pose of Mind Yoga: Do nothing ...

CHAPTER 4
MIND YOGA POSE 2: DO NOTHING

So far, you've taken a pretty big leap and tried Mind Yoga pose 1: Look inside. You've begun to see that the source of stress and even stress itself aren't what you once believed they were. Stress isn't coming from the outside, such as from a person, place, situation or event. It's only ever coming from our own thinking.

What do you do to try to manage and alleviate stress?

It could be anything from meditating to deep breathing, to attempting to think positively or change your mindset. You might drink more alcohol than you feel you should, or eat more food than is healthy for you. Write the list here or on another piece of paper.

Now, cross every item off the list. Every single one. Stop everything you're doing to manage stress (and it would be lovely to cross off the unhealthy habits, too).

I'm going to ask you to take an even bigger leap in Mind Yoga pose 2: Do nothing.

If you're meditating and exercising and you like the way you feel when you do them, then by all means keep doing those things. But if you're doing them as a way to alleviate stress, you can stop for that purpose.

If you're trying to manipulate your thoughts or feelings in any way to reduce stress, it's vital for you to stop. You're only adding more thinking into the mix, which is not helpful.

When I stopped everything I was doing to try to manage or stave off stress, stress began to fade into the background of my daily experience, all on its own.

Every message we receive about stress says we must do something about it, and everyone has a suggestion for what to do. But all the suggestions are coming at stress from the wrong direction because most people don't know that ...

a) stress is coming from our thinking, not from anything or anyone on the "outside";

b) we don't have to judge our thinking or see it as bad in some way, because everyone has this kind of thinking from time to time; and

c) stress moves out of the way quickly when we don't fear the feeling and allow thoughts to come and go, as they're designed to do.

Managing stress from the "outside" will never help.

As we talked about in chapters 2 and 3, stress only looks like it's coming from things on the outside. So changing jobs, trying to control events, dumping our significant other, moving to a new city, avoiding people we don't like and so forth may temporarily seem to fix things. But why do people have multiple relationships that all end the same way? Why do people change jobs and still feel miserable? Why do people move to a new city to escape stress – as I did once – and still feel stressed?

It's because circumstances and people have nothing to do with our feelings. **Our feelings reflect only our thinking in that particular moment, and nothing else.**

Therefore, the feeling we call "stress" is only mirroring our momentary thinking.

Key words here: momentary thinking. This will be significant in a few paragraphs, because if the feelings we call "stress" are coming only from our thoughts, then it seems to make sense to do something about our thoughts, right?

The simple answer is *No.*

We cannot control our thinking. There, I said it.

Do you know what you're going to be thinking thirty seconds from now, or even five seconds from now? Me neither. Whatever you may believe about controlling your thinking, it would be helpful for you to accept, starting now, that *there is nothing you can do to control your thinking*. It opens up a whole new world that's free of worrying about your thoughts. (You'll be amazed at the time that gets freed up, too.)

And here's the real kicker that is so obvious, I couldn't believe I missed it.

All the talk we hear about "changing our mindset" is leading us down the wrong path, too. Because once we've had a thought, it's too late to change it! "The horse is already out of the barn," as they say.

When you really look at thoughts in this way, it starts to seem quite funny to believe we can do anything about them. They happen randomly, at any time, with no warning. And then we're supposed to change or control them somehow?

Been there. Tried that for a couple dozen years.

Doesn't work.

Even if we somehow could control our thoughts, we don't need to "train our brain" to think better because a stress-free state is our natural setting.

A stress-free feeling, one of calm and peace, is our innate state as human beings. Don't believe me? That's OK. Just keep an open mind – pun intended – and continue reading ...

We can experience nearly instantaneous relief from any stress-inducing thinking if we let thoughts move on through our minds as they are designed to do, without interfering with them. Without trying to change our mindset. Without trying to think positively.

Trying to teach ourselves to think differently by reciting positive affirmations, for example, is part of an assumption that our minds (and us!) have an inherent problem that we have to fix. Nothing could be further from the truth.

For some reason, we believe that our minds work differently from our bodies. If we get a cut, we don't have to tell the cells how to mend the wound. They do it on their own.

Our mind functions the same way. Allow thoughts to come in and go out without trying to manipulate them, the mind settles down quickly, and we feel better.

When you observe your thoughts sometimes, you'll see that they come into your mind, and then they disappear. And we have thousands of thoughts every day that we're not even aware of. The only reason thoughts hang around more than a second or two is if we give them importance. We pluck old, stale thoughts out of the continual thought stream and randomly decide, "This is it! This is the thought that I need to pay attention to because it keeps coming around again! It must be important!"

You don't need to listen to old, stale thinking. It's not telling you anything useful. (In Mind Yoga pose 3, you'll see something far, far better that you can rely on.)

The mind works like a self-cleaning system that is continually bringing us fresh new thought.

Leave the system alone to do its thing, and unhelpful thoughts will be replaced by new and more helpful thoughts and accompanying good feelings.

Here's a big clue: Any feeling of distress means that we're believing that something on the outside is responsible for our stress, or we're listening to an old thought and believing that it's true. *The boss is a jerk. I will never be able to pay my bills. My life is horrible. If I could just get out of this marriage, my life would be perfect.*

None of it is true. It is thought, and it only looks true to us in that moment.

> We don't need to react to thoughts
> just because they go through our heads,
> especially if they're creating distress.

We're not obligated to do what thoughts tell us to do. We're not required to make them stop or go away, because they will do that all by themselves. **The more we stay out of the way, the faster we feel better.**

This is Mind Yoga pose 2: Do nothing.

Thanks to an understanding of what I'm sharing with you in this book, daily stress is no longer a problem for me. It honestly feels like some sort of miracle, especially considering how stressed I felt before. When I stopped everything I was doing to manage stress, my stress began to fade away.

But again, don't just believe me. Test it out. Try the simple Mind Yoga poses. See what happens.

You'll catch yourself believing that something on the "outside" is causing the feeling, and you'll say something like, "Oh, wait a minute. It's my thinking that's doing that, not my kids (or whatever it may be). Why do I need to be stressed out by my own thinking? That's kind of funny, actually."

The moment you see that it's thought and that you don't need to pay attention to it, is the moment that stress starts to fade away. This will take no effort on your part. See it once, and you'll see it again and again.

Do nothing. As strange as that sounds, it's the only real and lasting answer to stress.

Next up is my favorite of all the Mind Yoga poses ...

CHAPTER 5
MIND YOGA POSE 3: RELAX INTO CLARITY

So far, we've explored Mind Yoga pose 1: Look inside; and Mind Yoga pose 2: Do nothing.

Let's do a quick rewind on what we've seen so far.

Again, don't just accept what I'm saying. Test it for yourself and see what you discover.

With Mind Yoga pose 1, we looked in a new direction to see the true source of stress, which is always our thinking. It's not our thinking sometimes; it's our thinking every time. It's a fundamental principle, and it never varies, no matter how it might look to us.

In Mind Yoga pose 2, we've seen that doing nothing to manage stress is the fastest way for it to disappear. All we need "do" is see that we have thoughts and know that they will move along without us doing anything about them. We don't even have to see specific thoughts. It couldn't be any simpler than that.

Sometimes our thoughts create a stressful feeling. We don't need to fear the feeling our thoughts create. We do nothing and simply wait it out. The feeling passes quickly.

I know that looking inside and doing nothing seems completely counterintuitive compared to everything else we've been taught.

But that's the point of what I'm sharing in this book: up until now, what we've been told to do for stress doesn't work. Mind Yoga works because it's based on fundamental principles that few of us have ever been taught – until now.

You're probably asking, "That's all well and good. But how do I find answers to my problems, Mary? I still have them, even if I'm not being stressed by them."

That's what Mind Yoga pose 3 is all about: Relax into clarity. It's there where we can find the best answers to any problem we have.

Here's something that I'm guessing you've never heard before. It's a powerful promise.

Clarity and peace of mind are our natural state.

When I first came upon that statement a couple of years ago, I couldn't imagine that clarity and peace of mind were my default setting, my natural state as a human being. How could that be, after everything I had been through and all the stress I felt every day? Were all those experts really wrong? All those people who told me I was "mentally ill" with a stress disorder that I'd have to cope with forever?

I am happy to tell you that after experimenting time and again from a completely skeptical point of view, I have discovered that it is, in fact, true: clarity and peace are what we return to *if we do nothing to gain clarity and peace*. Ironic, isn't it?

The state we're trying to achieve by all this "managing" of stress is already present *when we do nothing at all.*

Spend any time listening to your thoughts, and you'll invariably hear the same ones over and over again. They sometimes remind me of static on the radio; I want to keep adjusting the knob to find the music underneath. If we have heard the same thoughts thousands of times, how can we expect to find new answers in them? We can't.

Yet that's what I used to do (and I'm guessing you do, too). I used to examine my thoughts, analyze my thoughts, try to figure out why I had certain thoughts. I turned my thoughts inside out, always looking for a new combination of thinking that would provide me with an answer. But what happened? I ended up back where I started, with a headful of static and stress and very little symphony.

Sometimes, though, I'd have an "a-ha!" moment. Usually it was when I wasn't doing anything related to the problem I wanted to solve. We typically get these "out of the blue" answers in the shower, while driving, while we're out for a walk or doing something we enjoy.

Wouldn't it be great to get those insights and new ideas more frequently and reliably? That's what Mind Yoga pose 3 helps us to do.

When our minds are clouded with old and stale thinking, it's difficult for any new ideas to come in. It's almost like they're a stack of rocks blocking the continual, fresh stream of thoughts that are available to us.

But when we see our old thinking for what it is and do nothing with it (Mind Yoga poses 1 and 2), those rocks dissolve instantly and the stream runs freely again.

Our minds are quieter, and our inner spaciousness rises to the surface. It's a place without constraints – and it's the source of those bright new ideas. Even when we're experiencing stressful thinking, clarity is always waiting for us just under the surface of our thoughts.

This is why Mind Yoga pose 3 is my favorite. It illustrates a truth that can not only change your relationship to stress, but it can also *transform your relationship to your life.*

When we see the simple fact that we think – not what we think, but *that* we think – we will begin to feel that spaciousness inside more often. I know it doesn't seem like the two things are connected, but they are.

Every time we see that our feelings are coming from our thoughts and not from something "out there," it's like we've pressed the "reset" button. We then experience our default setting of peace, calm and clarity. It's the wide-open space inside: a wellspring of new ideas, answers and solutions that surges up to meet us every time we ignore the static of our stressful thinking.

The only way for you to know that this is true is to experiment with it yourself. I'll show you how in a moment.

For me, the realization that clarity was my natural state was totally transformative. I went from seeing myself as a broken, unfixable person to deeply knowing that each one of us has everything we need, no matter how things may look to us based on our momentary thinking. I stopped questioning new ideas that came to me in times of clarity and began to trust myself more and more.

In short, this recognition of our natural state of well-being, peace and clarity absolutely changed my life. Not only did my stress dissolve away, but the outer circumstances of my life began to change without effort.

My relationships improved. I changed careers at age 54, and my professional life became much more rewarding. I have made many new friends, and opportunities have come along that would have been impossible for me to imagine, like meeting and working alongside people I've admired.

In the next chapter, I'll talk about how Mind Yoga can help you with any area of life in which you're feeling stressed.

Before I do, I invite you to try Mind Yoga for yourself the next time you feel even the slightest bit of stress. Do it as an experiment and see what happens.

Mind Yoga pose 1: See if you can connect that feeling of stress with your thoughts instead of attaching it to something or someone "out there." It's not the boss, the bad driver, your kids, your significant other, the job or anything else causing that uncomfortable feeling. It's your own thinking.

Even if you can't quite make that connection, please trust – even for just a moment – that that's actually what's happening.

I know it really looks like something on the "outside" is coming at us, but it never is. We're always feeling and experiencing the world of our own thinking, not a world "out there."

Here's an easy way to do this. If you're ever tempted to say, "I'm stressed because so-and-so did such-and-such (fill in the blank with your own details)," you know you're looking in the wrong direction. The only accurate and helpful way to complete that sentence is, "I'm stressed because I'm having stressful thinking, and I agree with it."

Usually that statement prompts a good laugh in me in that moment, and I bet it will with you, too. Because we don't have to agree with it!

Mind Yoga pose 2: Do nothing. You don't have to be afraid of the stressful feeling or worry about the fact that you're having stressful thinking. It's OK. Don't try to make it stop. Sit with it; wait it out. Don't react. Simply do nothing.

Mind Yoga pose 3: Relax into clarity. When the thoughts pass, which they always will when we leave them alone, so will the stressful sensation. Clarity emerges, and along with it, a better feeling, better ideas, and solutions to problems and challenges in your life.

How did it go? I'd love to hear, so please feel free to email me and let me know: mary@maryschiller.com.

Read on to discover how Mind Yoga can improve all areas of your life ...

CHAPTER 6
TRANSFORM YOUR LIFE WITH MIND YOGA

It may seem hard to believe that something as simple as Mind Yoga could impact not just the stress levels you're experiencing, but also things like your finances, your relationships, your creativity, your ability to make clear decisions, your productivity and more. In this chapter, I'll explain how this is possible by using real-life examples.

But first, let's review what's really happening when we feel stressed.

When we feel the sensation of stress, it means that in that particular moment, *we don't realize that the source of stress is our own thinking.* We're looking at something on the "outside" and believing that it is causing the stress.

I'll say this another way. Whenever I feel any kind of distress, I know it's because I've fallen into the illusion of my thinking. I'm believing that something "out there" is causing the feeling of stress, and I'm missing the fact that my distress is actually coming from listening to my own thinking.

Here is an example of how stress typically looks to us:

You wake up in the morning, and you're seized with stress and anxiety. You believe it's because you're out of a job and have bills to pay. Your heart is racing, and you're feeling a bit sick to your stomach. Today is the day you must find a job, or else!

You may try to calm down through deep breathing or by taking a walk around the block, but the feeling of stress keeps returning, and you know it will keep returning until you get a new job and have money to pay the bills. That's the only answer that looks like a solution, not only for the stress to stop but for your life to be OK.

You start to feel even more stressed as you peruse the job ads and send emails to everyone you know, hoping someone will offer you a job so that you can relax.

Sound familiar, even if the details change?

Here's how "stress" looks through the lens of Mind Yoga. I'll break it down as if it's occurring in super slow motion:

• You wake up in the morning, and you feel some physical sensations and strong emotions that are uncomfortable. You're in distress, so you know it's your thinking causing you to feel this way – because thinking is the only thing that ever causes feelings, including distress. You might catch a thought in mid-air – "I've got bills to pay! Aaaah!" – or you might just feel uncomfortable. (Mind Yoga pose 1: Look inside)

• You also know that your thoughts are random and could just as well be talking to you in Swahili (if you don't speak Swahili), especially when you've heard the same thoughts thousands of times before. (Mind Yoga pose 1: Look inside)

• You realize nothing on the "outside" needs to be dealt with right then for you to feel better, because nothing on the "outside" is causing this feeling. (Mind Yoga pose 1: Look inside)

• You sit with whatever the feeling is, realizing that it's coming from your momentary thinking and cannot hurt you. You don't worry about the feeling, the thinking or yourself. (Mind Yoga pose 2: Do nothing)

• The thought passes, and then the discomfort passes, and a sense of spaciousness and calm begins to emerge. (Mind Yoga pose 3: Relax into clarity)

• In that sense of spaciousness comes new, fresh thought, which holds an answer for you to get the bills paid – and even faster. (Mind Yoga pose 3: Relax into clarity)

Are you starting to see what a different experience – a different life – this understanding can create for you?

People I've coached in the principles behind Mind Yoga have come out of depression, been able to make clear decisions after feeling stuck (sometimes for years), approached difficult relationships from a new angle that promoted understanding instead of anger, increased their creative output, changed their focus from a job they dislike to passions they love, and more.

Let's look at a few examples of how your life, not just stress, can be transformed with Mind Yoga.

Financial stress can ease
with no change in your finances.

At one time or another, nearly everyone has experienced stress related to finances. I am no exception. For years, I was preoccupied with worry over money. I was constantly stressed about how much money my husband and I were earning, how much debt we were carrying, how little we had saved for retirement, and on and on. I even talked about money incessantly. What a bore I must have been!

When I came upon the principles that underscore Mind Yoga, I was astonished at what I saw. So much of my time each day was taken up by thoughts about money: half my waking hours, at least. I couldn't believe it. It freaked me out.

Then I began to understand that my "money stress" wasn't about money at all. I didn't have a money problem; I had a thinking problem. That was Mind Yoga pose 1, look inside. I saw that my stress was coming from my own thoughts, not from how much money was in the bank. Looking back on my life, I could see that what had looked like the ups and downs of money stress were actually fluctuating thinking, not a fluctuating bank account.

In the past, I had tried to ease the stress I felt around money by trying to change my thinking. I even took a (rather expensive, ironically) course to change my "money mindset." Needless to say, it didn't work. It was obvious why, too: my thoughts weren't the problem. By following that money-mindset program, I was trying to manipulate my thinking, but I was still listening to my thinking!

So this time, instead of trying to change my thinking about money, I began to adopt Mind Yoga pose 2: Do nothing.

I simply saw that I was thinking about money, and that's it. I also realized that I could turn my inner gaze away from that thinking instead of trying to change it. Although it wasn't easy at first because those thoughts were so mesmerizing and pervasive, it worked. The less I did to try to change or eliminate these thoughts, the quicker they faded into the distance and the more at ease I felt no matter how much money I had in the bank.

Can you guess what began to happen next? As the stress began to dissolve, the easier it was for me to create new career opportunities – exciting ways to really enjoy my work and make money at the same time. As I'm writing this book, I've had a complete career change and have been able to develop a profitable business with very little effort.

It makes sense: I'm not preoccupied with worrying about money anymore, so solutions are appearing in the space that was freed up when those anxious thoughts faded away. Even more importantly, I recognize that my security isn't tied to how much money I have in the bank. It's part of that default setting we learned about in Mind Yoga pose 3. Abundance, clarity, security and well-being are always available to us. They're part of the package of simply being a human being.

What I have seen, and what you can see, too, is that no amount of money has the power to either give us security or cause us stress. We can be happy and successful with five dollars in the bank or with five million dollars in the bank.

Mind Yoga pose 1: Look inside. See that whatever feeling you have is always coming from your own momentary thinking, not from a dollar figure in your bank account or on a bill – even when it doesn't look this way. The illusion of our thinking can be very convincing. Trust that it is an illusion and see what happens.

Mind Yoga pose 2: Do nothing. The simple truth is that there is nothing for you to do to ease the stress. The system of thought is designed to help you if you allow your thoughts to move along on their own, and that includes worrisome thoughts about money.

Mind Yoga pose 3: Relax into clarity. You'll open up to endless possibilities for how to create the money you'd like to have because your stressful thinking fades into the distance, leaving you space to see what you couldn't see before.

How might your life transform if you weren't worried about money? I don't mean that you'd magically have a million dollars in the bank tomorrow (although who knows?). I mean that whatever anxiety or concern you had related to money simply wasn't there anymore. What might you accomplish with the time that's freed up when those worries are gone? Write out your ideas here or on another piece of paper.

Stressful relationships can be improved with Mind Yoga.

Wow, did I ever have a lot of relationship stress a while back. For several years, my current husband and I traveled a rocky road. We even separated for a time, and we felt about as far apart emotionally as two people could be. He was dealing with depression, and I was facing the stress I talked about in chapter 1 of this book. It was not a good combination for a healthy and happy relationship.

To top it off, there was something I used to believe in, something I did, that honest to goodness was almost the death of my marriage. Granted, as I just mentioned, there were a few other factors that were keeping us skating on the edge of divorce. But this was a big part of it.

I wanted to talk about everything.

I wanted to "talk things out." I wanted to "leave no stone unturned." I wanted to "not let the sun set on my anger."

You know what it was? Well intentioned, but wrong.

We're told that talking is the way to help fix a relationship. Knowing what I know now, I can see that it's not about talking, but about something else entirely.

It's about connecting non-judgmentally with another human being. About seeing them for who they really are. And talking when the time is right, and then saying very little.

But I saw something else, too:

- My husband wasn't hurting my feelings.
- My husband wasn't treating me in a way that I deserved, or didn't deserve.
- My husband's behavior – whatever it happened to be – wasn't a response to me or my behavior.

For example, sometimes I thought my husband and I weren't getting along because I wasn't worth his love. When he forgot to give me a gift on a special day, for instance, I took it personally and believed it was intentional.

It never occurred to me that it could have been an oversight. I thought I didn't deserve a gift, anyway, so maybe he was right not to give me something. And then I'd get angry and think he was just a thoughtless person. It was a vicious and destructive cycle.

When I began to see what was really going on, it was as if a whole new version of my husband, of myself, and of our relationship began to materialize. Imagine an out-of-focus photograph gradually becoming crystal clear. That's how it felt to me. I saw that his behavior and my feelings had no relationship – pun intended – to one another.

How does all this relate to Mind Yoga? I recognized that my feelings came from my own thinking, not from anything my husband was or wasn't doing.

That was pose 1: Look inside.

The next phase of my understanding was recognizing that I didn't have to do anything, and my husband didn't have to do anything, for my feelings to change.

That was pose 2: Do nothing.

The most beautiful phase of this understanding was when I began to relax into clarity, pose 3 of Mind Yoga.

As clarity emerged within me, the quality and timing of my conversations with my husband began to improve. Instead of reacting to momentary thinking that caused me distress, I'd wait for the distress to pass. Usually by that time, I was seeing him, and our relationship, completely differently: with clarity and understanding instead of anger and frustration. Often I'd forget what I'd been upset about.

My ability to connect with him – of seeing through the surface stress he was under because of his own thinking – deepened immeasurably.

Then, the stress levels in our household dropped precipitously. We stopped arguing. There was a peaceful silence when before, there was tension and turmoil.

And all it took was me, not even both of us at first.

I saw what was actually creating my own experience – the simple understanding that forms the three poses of Mind Yoga. Gradually, my husband, too, became aware of the principles of Mind Yoga, and now the two of us are on this journey together.

If you have a relationship with someone that is challenging and stressful – be it with a family member, colleague, boss, child, significant other – how might things change for you if that stress dissolved? What would you love to see happen as a result of that stress going away? Write out your ideas here or on a separate piece of paper.

Creativity, productivity and decision making become much simpler.

I'd like you to take a few moments and consider how much of your day is spent in stressful thinking.

Remember, we're talking about your stressful thinking, not stress coming from "out there" – because stress never comes from anything or anyone "out there" (that's Mind Yoga pose 1: look inside).

How much of your day is spent ...

- Worrying about an unknowable future?

- Ruminating on events of the past?

- Criticizing yourself?

- Thinking about what other people should or shouldn't be doing?

- Concerning yourself with others' opinions of you?

- Guessing as to the causes of other people's behavior?

- Imagining what your life would be like "if only [fill in the blank] would happen"?

What if you could reclaim that time? That's what Mind Yoga can do for you. It will give you your time back.

Mind Yoga can give you your life back.

When we see the truth about stress, we realize that we no longer have to try to control or fix anything "out there." And when we understand the principles of Mind Yoga, we also know that we don't have to try to control of fix anything "in here," inside our minds, because there's nothing to fix.

The human system is designed to work on our behalf, returning us to clarity when we allow it to do its thing.

Without those two tasks – trying to fix things "out there" and trying to fix our own thinking – hanging over us all the time, can you imagine what kind of space is created? For me, the sensation is one of endless possibility, like I'm looking at an infinite vista of wide-open land – something like the state of Montana, perhaps (although I have never personally visited that beautiful place, so it's how I imagine it).

Even though it might appear that decision making could be more complex – with all those choices and possibilities, how do I choose? – just the opposite is true. Decisions become so clear that they don't feel like decisions. There is no relentless weighing of options. I'm sure you've had this experience before, when a choice is so obvious it's like no other exists.

That's the kind of experience you can have routinely with Mind Yoga.

As for me, I no longer pay attention to thinking related to trauma or money, for example. Just with those two topics out of the way, my productivity and creativity have increased to the point where it often feels like I've gained several hours in the day. My creative output is higher quality, and my coaching work with clients is more focused and effective.

As a result, I have more time to spend with people I love and doing other activities I enjoy. And during leisure time, I'm truly "unplugged" from distractions.

What do you want more time for?

When you begin to de-stress your life with Mind Yoga, you'll have time and space in your life again – or maybe for the first time ever. What would you like to do with that time? Write out your ideas here or on a separate of paper.

I want you to know that as your understanding of Mind Yoga deepens, your life will begin to transform in the best way possible – and with no effort on your part. Something I've seen over and over again is that just a glimpse behind the curtain into the cause and solution for stress is enough for people's lives to change. In that way, you are no exception – and that's a beautiful thing.

Let's do one final review of the Mind Yoga poses.

Mind Yoga pose 1: Look inside. See that stress only comes from listening to our own thinking, not from anything on the "outside" of us. This phrase helps me see this more easily: "I'm stressed because I'm having stressful thinking, and I agree with it." (Laughing at oneself always breaks the spell!)

Mind Yoga pose 2: Do nothing. The mind is designed to work like a self-cleaning system. When we don't interfere – when we stop trying to manipulate or change our thinking, which we can't do, anyway – the system moves us from stress to calm quite quickly. We don't have to be afraid of any stressful feelings we might have because nothing on the "outside" is causing them.

We don't need to fix anything at all, because nothing is broken – including us.

Mind Yoga pose 3: Relax into clarity. The feeling of peace, spaciousness and clarity is our natural state as human beings. The only reason we don't experience it more often is because we get caught up in our thoughts sometimes. That's not a judgment of any kind; it's simply part of being a human being. But feeling calm is also our birthright, the place of equilibrium to which we return time and again, without fail.

You must have a few questions, so I'll provide answers …

Chapter 7
Frequently Asked Questions

Q. Is Mind Yoga anything like the Law of Attraction or other self-development or self-help tools and techniques?

A. No. All you need "do" is see that you're thinking, and that your thinking is creating your experience of stress. Once you see that nothing outside of you is creating stress, the misunderstanding is gone, and the stress fades away. You don't have to try to change or control your thinking in any way (because no one can do that).

We don't have to attract good feelings and abundance into our lives. Why would we have to attract something that we already have? The answer is that we don't. We already have everything. We already *are* everything. That's what becomes so apparent with Mind Yoga pose 3: Relax into clarity. We start to see how many resources already exist within us to create what we'd love to experience in this life.

Q. Did you come up with Mind Yoga all on your own, Mary?

A. Mind Yoga is my interpretation of the insights of Sydney Banks and his expression of those insights as the Three Principles of Mind, Consciousness and Thought. Since I have personally seen how much those principles have helped me alleviate stress, I wanted to create a simple way for people to help dissolve their own stress, too. So I developed Mind Yoga.

Q. What really makes Mind Yoga so different?

A. It is not prescriptive. It is descriptive. It is not telling us to do anything; in fact, it's just the opposite. It is simply showing us what is really going on.

Once we see how things work, we can begin living with true freedom and, of course, a whole lot less stress.

Q. Can Mind Yoga help with physical or chronic pain?

A. Yes. Even our experience of physical distress comes to us via our own thinking. In my own case, I have noticed that when I don't give any weight to worrisome thinking about my physical state when I'm ill or in pain, the pain often subsides quickly. I'm also clearer if I have to make a medical-related decision. As I mentioned, I have a chronic problem with my spine. In the past, before I understood the principles behind Mind Yoga, I would spend weeks in pain. Since gaining this new understanding, I have had far fewer problems and when it has flared up, the pain has lasted only a day or two.

Q. Are there more poses in Mind Yoga?

A. The principles that form the foundation of Mind Yoga offer endless possibilities for exploration. For me, that's the best part. The rest of my life will be an exciting journey into the clarity and peace that I longed for and didn't realize I already had within me.

Q. So if I don't have to do anything, well ... I'm confused. Then what do I do?

A. Nothing. You have innate well-being and clarity. When you see that there is nothing outside of you creating stress, and that it's all coming from within you, it's like you've pressed the "reset" button on your whole system: a system that is always tilting in the direction of health and a stress-free state.

In other words, even though you're not aware of it, you are always conspiring to help ... you!

Q. If I understand Mind Yoga, does that mean I'll never feel stressed again?

A. You'll still have those feelings sometimes because that's part of the human experience. We have thoughts; those thoughts instantly create certain feelings, like stress.

But here's the difference: *you don't need to worry about having those feelings* because they're simply reflecting your thinking in the moment, and that's all. Your feelings don't mean anything more than that. They're not a reflection of who you are or how well or badly your life is going.

Your feelings only ever do that one thing: reflect thought in the moment. Feel the feeling, of stress or whatever it is, and wait it out. Don't be afraid of it. It can't hurt you. A new feeling will come along in a moment. When you understand the true source of stress, that new feeling will be a much more beautiful one every single time. Your experience of "stress" will be short lived and will no longer have any power over you.

Q. I want to learn more about the principles behind Mind Yoga. How do I do that?

A. I'm always available to answer questions, and I offer regular classes in Mind Yoga, both in person and online. You can find me at www.maryschiller.com.

What's next? I'd love for you to …

CHAPTER 8
SHARE MIND YOGA

People deserve to feel less stress in their lives – including you and those you love and care about. It's my dream to share Mind Yoga with as many people as possible because I truly believe that the world can be a happier and more peaceful place. You can help me share the joy around the globe just by telling one person about Mind Yoga.

1. Your review of this short book on Amazon or wherever you purchased it (thank you!) would be so appreciated. Many, many thanks.

2. If this book has been valuable to you, please share it in a post, blog or tweet, or give a copy of this book to a friend or loved one. You might find people in your workplace, your neighborhood, your place of worship or your child's school who could benefit, too.

3. Find me online at www.maryschiller.com to learn more about Mind Yoga classes and personalized coaching. I'd love to have a conversation with you about having less stress and far more joy and ease in your life.

Thank you for reading and sharing *Mind Yoga*.

Much love to you,
Mary

THE END ... OF STRESS

ABOUT THE AUTHOR

Mary Schiller, creator of Mind Yoga (and self-proclaimed Mind Yoga Master), is a coach who helps people experience more joy, relaxation and clarity in their lives.

She is also the author of *The Joy Formula: The simple equation that will change your life.*

Before she began teaching people Mind Yoga, Mary taught university students how to write the perfect essay. Later, she became a communications officer at Columbia University, crafting messages for the business and medical schools. She holds advanced degrees in English and in education.

A native Californian, Mary loves the sun and the surf but also enjoys traveling to Paris and sampling every delicacy in the patisserie. She's passionate about classical music (Beethoven is unmatched), art, photography and knitting, particularly sweaters. She's married and has a grown daughter plus two adorable cats. While Mary and her husband currently live in New York City, they may be making a move soon to Europe. Wherever she may be, you can find and connect with Mary online at www.maryschiller.com.

Made in the USA
Middletown, DE
15 June 2023